The Boy Who Said Wow

by
Todd Boss

art by
Rashin Kheiriyeh

BEACH LANE BOOKS
New York London Toronto Sydney New Delhi

For Ronan and his family—T. B.

To my nephew, Armin, whom I love so much.
I wish a beautiful life for neurodivergent kids
all over the world.—R.K.

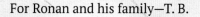

BEACH LANE BOOKS • An imprint of Simon & Schuster Children's Publishing Division • 1230 Avenue of the Americas, New York, New York 10020 •
Text © 2020 by Todd Boss • Illustration © 2024 by Rashin Kheiriyeh • Book design © 2024 by Simon & Schuster, Inc. • The text of this book was originally
broadcast as an episode of the *Classical Kids Storytime* program on Minnesota Public Radio. • All rights reserved, including the right of reproduction in
whole or in part in any form. • BEACH LANE BOOKS and colophon are trademarks of Simon & Schuster, Inc. • Simon & Schuster: Celebrating 100 Years
of Publishing in 2024 • For information about special discounts for bulk purchases, please contact Simon & Schuster Special Sales at 1-866-506-1949 or
business@simonandschuster.com. • The Simon & Schuster Speakers Bureau can bring authors to your live event. For more information or to book an
event, contact the Simon & Schuster Speakers Bureau at 1-866-248-3049 or visit our website at www.simonspeakers.com. • The text for this book was
set in PT Serif Pro. • The illustrations for this book were rendered in watercolor, ink, acrylic, chalk, and collages. • Manufactured in China • 1123 SCP •
First Edition • 10 9 8 7 6 5 4 3 2 1 • Library of Congress Cataloging-in-Publication Data • Names: Boss, Todd, author. | Kheiriyeh, Rashin,
illustrator. • Title: The boy who said wow / Todd Boss ; illustrated by Rashin Kheiriyeh. • Description: First edition. | New York : Beach Lane Books,
[2023] | Audience: Ages 4-8. | Audience: Grades 2-3. | Summary: When Ronan, a nonverbal boy, goes to the symphony, the beautiful music moves him to
speak. • Identifiers: LCCN 2022046898 (print) | LCCN 2022046899 (ebook) | ISBN 9781534499713 (hardcover) | ISBN 9781534499720 (ebook) • Subjects:
CYAC: Mutism—Fiction. | Concerts—Fiction. | Music—Fiction. | LCGFT: Picture books. • Classification: LCC PZ7.1.B6744 Bo 2023 (print) | LCC PZ7.1.B6744
(ebook) | DDC [E]—dc23 • LC record available at https://lccn.loc.gov/2022046898 • LC ebook record available at https://lccn.loc.gov/2022046899

"What a beautiful morning,"
 says Father.
"Shall we go to the beach?"

Ronan is quiet.

"What a lovely afternoon," says Mother.
"Shall we go to the park?"

Ronan is quiet.

Suddenly, Grandfather
bursts through the door.
"Let's go to a concert!"

"A risk!" says Mother.

"A challenge!" says Father.

"An adventure!" cries Grandfather.

Ronan is quiet as he gets into the car.

He is quiet as they leave the sleepy countryside.

The city is noisy.
Grandfather is noisy too.
He talks and talks and talks.

But Ronan is quiet
all the way to Symphony Hall.

Some children are born noisy,
but Ronan was born quiet.
Some days he hardly says a word.

What goes on in his head, do you suppose?
Only Ronan knows.

"What a fantastic concert hall," says Ronan's grandfather as they take their seats.

Ronan is quiet
as the musicians come onstage.

Ronan is quiet
as the lights go down.
Everyone is quiet now.
The music is about to begin.

And then it does!

The darker instruments
sound cool and frightening.

ZUMMITY
ZUMMITY
ZIM

The lighter instruments sound warm and friendly.

Together they sound
like a sky full of stars.

Now the music is done.
Everything is silent. The stars fade away.

Then Ronan's mouth opens
and out comes a great, big . . .

This WOW isn't just any old WOW.
It's Ronan's first WOW!
  It fills up Ronan's whole face.
  It fills up the hearts of all the people in the audience!

It fills up the whole concert hall!

Everybody laughs!
Then everybody claps!

They are clapping for the orchestra . . .

and they are clapping for Ronan, too!

Ronan is quiet
all the way home.

Ronan is quiet
as he's tucked into bed.

"Wow," whispers Mother.
"Wow," whispers Father.

Shhhhh.
Quiet, now.

Ronan may still
be listening. . . .

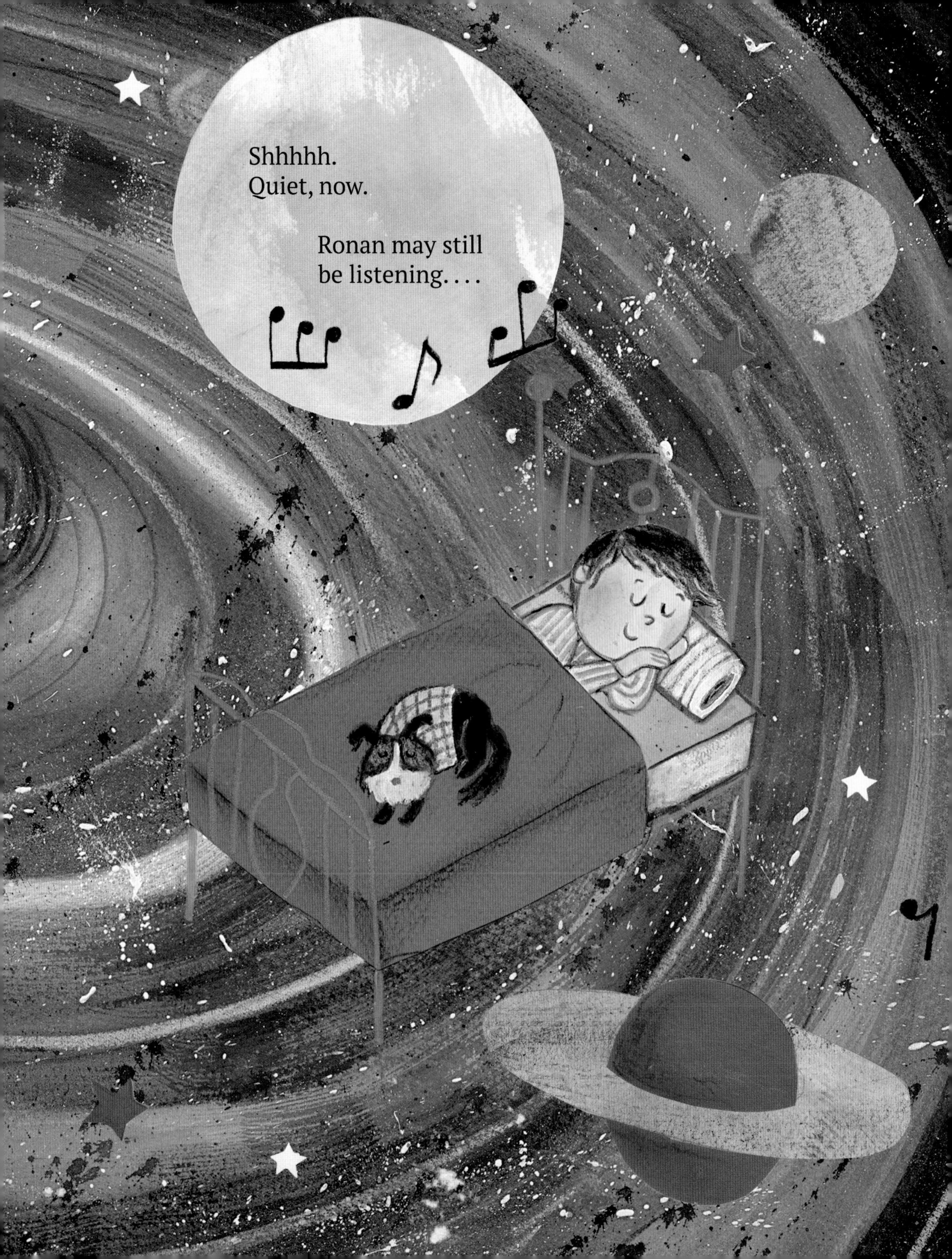

This story really happened.

On May 5, 2019, at Boston's Symphony Hall, a nine-year-old boy named Ronan Mattin broke the silence after a performance of Mozart's *Masonic Funeral Music* by the Handel and Haydn Society with a "Wow!" that echoed throughout the hall and inspired laughter, cheers, and applause. Ronan is nonverbal, which means he usually doesn't speak much. But that night, he seemed to speak for everyone in the audience, and his "Wow!" was caught on a radio recording that was heard around the world.